Restoring the Brokenness

Bishop Theadore E. Payne Sr.

Publisher's Name: Bishop Theadore E. Payne Sr.

ISBN: 978-1-971601-20-5
eBook ISBN: 978-1-971601-21-2

TABLE OF CONTENTS

Introduction iv

Acknowledgement vi

Endorsements vii

Chapter 1: History/ His Story 1

Chapter 2: A family that will pray together 7

Chapter 3: Deliver the enemy from within 14

Chapter 4: Laughing to Scorn 21

Chapter 5: Discovering the Treasure Inside 29

Chapter 6: Confidence 36

Chapter 7: Divine Healing 44

Introduction

The ultimate purpose of writing this book was inspired by God, my family and friends, and also because of the passion I have to see people restored back to their rightful place into the kingdom of God. Remember when the prodigal son left home; he received, he returned, he repented, then he was restored. God desires to restore your broken spirit today, restore your health and everything that has been taken from you.

Each of us has had some sort of vicissitude in our lives that has been detrimental to the success or failure of what God has called us to do. Please don't let anything or anyone deter you from reaching your destiny which God has preordained just for you.

I have been so compassionate about this topic that in 2011, our ministry included the word "Restoration" in the name. Oak Grove Baptist Church is now referred to as Oak Grove Baptist Restoration Ministries. Oak Grove is the name of the community and Baptist is significant to our ancestors, yet we realize that God is not interested with denomination. He is very interested with our relationship with Him. I believe that God is very concerned that His church has a true heart to see others restored; those that are lame, blind, withered, emaciated, wounded, or broken. He wants to see those that are broken be totally restored to the fullness of God's intention.

My life is represented in every chapter of this little book. Therefore, it is my prayer that something in this book will illuminate that specific area in your life, thus encourage you to know that God is restoring you at this very moment!

Acknowledgement

*T*hanks to the love of my life, my wife, Gwendolyn Darnice Fitzpatrick Payne, our lovely children, TJ and Goldie, Jonathan and Sonya Mark and Kera including our precious grandchildren and great grandchild.

To my spiritual sons and daughters, thank you.

Thanks to our entire family and church family, some of you have been with me from the very beginning of this tour of life. Thanks for allowing this broken, yet restored vessel to serve as your pastor.

Thanks to my spiritual fathers, Bishops, Pastors and Mothers that have sown the word of God into my life, which has caused me to be where I am today.

Endorsements

Theadore Payne is one of the finest leaders I know. He has that rare combination of a humble spirit and a fully yielded heart and full of wisdom. The story of his life as told by him in this book is both enlightening and entertaining. His heart for the restoration of God's people and communities are both heartwarming and inspiring. He has a desire to see people redeemed, healed, and set free from their afflictions and reached their full potential in Christ. The Church for the 21st Century will require a higher level of leadership and compassion than ever before in history. Leaders like Bishop Payne will contribute greatly to ushering in this new era of leadership.

I am grateful for Theadore Payne, for his friendship and the impact that he is having on churches and leaders in his city and surrounding areas. This is a great read for anyone desiring to hear the voice from a great man of God.

Eugene V. Reeves - Bishop prelate of the Eagles Rock of the Communion of Christian leaders

It is my privilege to know and be in fellowship with Bishop Payne for a few years. He and his family are some of the sweetest people I know. Bishop is a physically big man but his heart is even bigger. It was my privilege to consecrate Pastor Payne to the office of Bishop and he impressed me in his willingness to devour all the books

I recommended. This combination of heart and head makes him a compassionate academic.

Bishop Payne is a genuine shepherd who watches over the people of God with great conviction and commitment. He is as well a devoted husband and father and these observations continue to impress me. His ministry in the local church and community continues to bring honor and glory to God.

In the introduction of his book Bishop Payne draws us in with his moving and inspiring personal testimony and then releases the power of God to restore all those in need. I recommend this book as a **must read** for all who wish to be made whole.

Congratulations Bishop, job well done.

The Right Reverend Doctor Van B. Gayton

Chapter 1

History/ His Story

For I will restore health to you and will heal you whom no one seeks after and for whom no one cares! (Amplified Version)

Dan B. Allender once stated and I quote "The work of restoration cannot begin until a problem is fully faced"

God has great thoughts toward us as His children and I am so glad that when He saw me in His mind, He saw peace and not evil. Therefore, the eschatological days of my life were pre planned and placed on God's heart, regardless of when I was conceived. Before my parents and family members were ever able to speak to me, hold me, or even rock me to sleep, God knew my beginning from my ending.

Let it be known, since the fall of man, which was caused by the decision of Adam & Eve, restoration has been on the very heart of God. He has a plan for us, a plan of good and not of evil and especially from the perspective of the outcast; those that the world would have counted out for the count, out as a failure and considered not good enough for this current world system.

I am sure that I have not always felt like an outcast, but those days of uncertainty perhaps began at a very young age for me. My problematic life as a child began to be difficult between the period of four and five years of age. At that time, we didn't have inside bathrooms, so we had to use the outside facility (if you know what I mean). I considered it a long distance from our home. While I was in that outdoor facility one day, a thunder storm arose suddenly and boisterously. At that moment, I quickly left that building and I began running towards our home. The lightning and thunder was extremely loud! It scared me so badly that I felt as though I had been hit with lightning, which caused me to begin to slip and slide up the grass incline. At that time; as I was thinking in my heart, so was I.

I looked up toward our home place and all I could see was my grandfather and family members in the door way. My grandfather, standing at 6'3", was coming for me with his huge hands reaching out toward me to lift me up. This is just like God; our God will never leave us alone in a storm! However, from that moment on, I begin feeling unusually nervous and uncertain which then opened a door to the difficulty in my speech. But I believe regardless of our situation, God can always turn things around for our good!

During all of this, regardless of my difficulty, my family had never laughed at me or ever made fun of my situation. They cared about what I was going through and loved me unconditionally. Yet my inside was unbalanced, mentally and emotionally challenged. My heart was strong and my spirit was willing; but with the continued challenge in my speech, I felt less than.

How am I going to handle reading the Sunday school lesson at church? How will I give my report in elementary school? How could I read in front of others, much less to think considering my future in high school? These types of questions began to consume my mind, even at this very young age.

Now I'm in the first grade and there were two separate buildings that housed six classes, 1st through the 6th grade. Three classes were in each building and there were not any room dividers. The students were only separated by rows for each class. In today's society, that would be unheard of! But due to this arrangement of the classes, everybody would hear me stutter. Of course when it was my turn to read or speak, I was extremely nervous. But my elementary teacher, Mrs. Nicholas, was a very special little lady with freckles who was loveable, considerate and fluffy. She may have been short in structure, but she had a huge heart as an educator. God had me on His mind when he assigned her to be my teacher.

Mrs. Nicholas had a unique style of teaching. It was one that everyone could understand together and no one would be embarrassed, feel less than, or left out.

When it came to math, she taught it differently. She would lead it off by saying, "one and one is two". But she did this not only by just writing it on the chalk board; but While she would be explaining it, she would be singing it. Singing math; wow, what a concept!

This teaching method made the lesson to be in a harmonious form and I found out I could do that. I was able to sing it with everyone else without stuttering and this made my challenge become relatively easy.

Now it's reading time and we would read about Sally, Dick, Jane and Spot. You are probably familiar with that little small paperback book.

Everyone in the class was now learning how to read in the same fashion, singing, and that was just perfect for me. Maybe this is also what started developing my appreciation to minister through song.

Our God is so awesome that because we are the apple of His eye, God always has a ram in the bush. A ram that can be a sacrifice for us, that reflects on God's goodness and his appreciation for His children.

This system continued into the next group of classes, 4th through the 6th grade and these classes were a little more difficult. I became apprehensive about studying; because that would mean after I completed the 6th grade and was promoted, I would be going to another school.

Those elementary school days had served as a state of comfort for me. Now being faced with the challenge of being promoted to the next level, including going to another school in the city, to me was scary. So for two grades, fear over took me which created boundaries in my education. But God!

I felt comfortable in that little two room school system because they all knew me and they understood me. I became conformed to my environment. I was losing the drive to study because eventually when I would pass to the next grade, I would be transferred to a larger school. A school filled with people that I didn't know. Imagining they would be smarter, faster and more advanced, I lost the ambition and drive to succeed for two complete years. I didn't care if I passed to the next grade or not. Fear had over taken me, even though we all realize that the acronym of FEAR is False Evidence Appearing Real!

The enemy almost conquered my life, but as the Apostle Paul stated it in the book of Romans; we are not just conquerors, but more than conquerors!

When I finally made it to high school, it was more challenging. But I had made up my mind that I was going to study and show myself approved, so that I wouldn't be humiliated or ashamed. My grades turned around, little by little, my confidence was getting stronger. There was a new young lad on the horizon that was trying to come out.

During the summer of my high school years, I was employed at a service garage. I was trained to recondition and restore vehicles that the customers would trade in. They were usually dirty, with dull paint, rusty. To some, their vehicles would have been considered an outcast and embarrassed to drive. But after those automobiles were completely cleaned up, it was always amazing to observe how they appeared once they were restored! You could even see what color the original paint was on the engine after it was steamed off from the years' buildup of grease and oil. The carpet and seats would be cleaned or re-covered. Later, when we would place that automobile on the car lot, it looked like it did when it was first purchased. Often the original owners would return for various reasons, then look at their old car and not believe that was the same vehicle.

That job at the garage taught me that regardless of what we may look like at this present moment, on the inside or the outside; we can always be restored and better than ever before.

That is what others think when they see us after God has restored us, that we are better than before. I have often heard words like, "I can't believe you are the same person".

Little did I know that God was setting me up for my destiny? Life as we know it today is only a set up for a greater future. Restoration is the act of restoring, renewal, reviving and or reestablishment; so please allow God to begin his work of restoration in you.

Chapter 2

A family that will pray together

He shall call upon me, and I will answer him: I will be with him in trouble;
I will deliver him, and honour him. Psalms 91:15 (KJV)

The first seven years of an individual's life is the foundation for the rest of their existence. It is that foundation that holds the key to successful and victorious living. My grandfather died when I was seven years of age. Watching my grandfather's life was the good foundation that I needed to teach me how to be a believer, a man, a father, a provider and a grandfather. It also taught me how to be faithful. He was the only man that I knew and saw daily in our home growing up, and what a great example he was for me. I really missed him but what I was able to glean from his life still lingers with me until this present moment.

My grandfather was somebody that I loved dearly and his character was symbolic of how God provides for his children. ***James 1:17 states, "Every good gift and every perfect gift is from above***" KJV. Just as God loves to bless His children, my grandfather also loved to give to us. He always had us on his mind. It seemed like every week he would bring a gift, a toy, a treat, candy or some sort of item that indicated that he often thought of us.

One week, he bought each of us a rocking chair, plus one table to share among us. During our playtime, my sisters would sit down at the table pretending to be the congregation and I was appointed to be the preacher? I would immediately ask myself, “Who me”? Do they really want me to preach? The very first funeral service I performed was for one of our pigs that had died and all of us attended. It was only a few words given, but I completed the service. Expecting laughter from them, I received something very different. It was their support. They didn’t seem to mind because we were only children and they were my sisters. My mother and grandmother were usually in the kitchen cooking something that always had a great aroma. Their occupation was cooking and often I could smell the meals being prepared with such love and appreciation, which were characteristics of our home

Over the course of time, the chairs that my grandfather purchased began to fall apart. My chair was in the worst shape and I wasn’t content with that. I located the best chair of the group and claimed it to be mine by grabbing an old hairpin from my mother’s collection and scratching the back of that particular chair. Hmmm, I guess this was a little bit of Jacob represented in me. Like me, Jacob had also claimed something to be his that didn’t rightfully belong to him by cheating his older brother out of his blessing in Genesis 27.

Several years ago, my step father lost his life in a fire that completely destroyed our home place. All of our personal belongings and lifetime of possessions were also destroyed in that fire. But today, I have that same chair from my grandfather in our current home and it is the only piece of furniture left out of everything that was in our home then. "WOW", what an heirloom! It will always remind me of those times when my sisters and I would play church and how that was a foreshadowing of my future as a preacher.

On Sunday mornings before breakfast was served, we would have family prayer. Someone in the family would read a scripture and then most of the time my grandmother would pray. My grandmother prayed in such a manner that she would begin by talking to God, but before the prayer would end the talking would be transformed into a moaning. It sounded like singing and yet calling on the name of the Lord at the same time. You don't hear of folks praying like that anymore, but I was beginning to see a pattern being formed in my life. My prayer life was being established.

Going to church during this period in my life, I would hear the old preachers preach inspiring messages. When they would reach the height of their messages or they were in their high moments, usually near the closing, the preaching would begin to sound like music. Was it singing or was it preaching? To many, it is a term called hooping. Nevertheless, I could understand it and connected to it.

God knows how to take the simple things in life to teach and instruct us. These are the things that usually would have been overlooked by others. God uses the simplicity of life's issues to place us in position for restoration. Through this process, He will ultimately turn our mourning into dancing. I believe that regardless of our situation, God can turn it around for our good?

We spent our entire childhood in that home but as a family growing up, we seldom ever argued with each other. Most people who I have shared this with, found it unbelievable to know that a brother and sisters can live together and never argue. However, this was a true statement in our case. Unfortunately, I lost my youngest sister several years ago. She unexpectedly had a massive heart attack at the young age of 48. In all the years we've lived and grew up together, it is difficult to count the number of times on one hand that we ever had any disagreements or arguments over anything. We loved and appreciated each other for who we were. Growing up with true love for each other was truly a wonderful gift. We just trusted one another and were in complete support of each other in everything that we encountered. Undeniably, it was that love and support of my family that helped me through countless adversities.

By this time, singing has now become a part of my personal life. My sisters and I would often sing at home for ourselves, but one day we were asked to sing on the youth hour program at our church. The plan was that I would lead off the song, ***"To me, it is so wonderful to***

know that Jesus is mine". I opened my mouth to begin singing, but nothing came out. This was supposed to be an opportunity to demonstrate to the community, the singing that we did at home. However, things were not working out the way it was intended.

I closed my eyes as I continued to attempt singing the song. And when I finally got the nerve to reopen them, I saw a couple of individuals sitting near the front of the church who found this incident to be comical. But to me, it was very embarrassing. The first line of the song seemed to have taken ten minutes. Looking at them, I continued to force those words out until the song was complete. I was still embarrassed, but I felt that God was with me. I only knew one verse and the chorus at that time. But when I recently listened to the entire song, my eyes began to well up because there was a heartfelt message there just for me.

"When I should feel lonely or I should feel sad, I'll go to the Lord and He'll make me feel glad; joy bells are ringing, my soul is singing, to know that Jesus is mine".

So just because things don't go well the first time, does not indicate that it is not your gift. God places talents and gifts inside of us but sometimes we need to be groomed and prepared. God used that laughter to push that gift out of me! I was then asked to sing that same song at our neighboring churches at other times. It seemed like the more I sang it, the more comfortable I became. From that time on, I have been asked to minister through song numerous times until this present day.

Proverbs 18:16 ¶ a man's gifts makes room for him, And brings him before great men (NKJV)

At a young age, I would occasionally walk to the church in our community and pray before going to school. This is where I felt God's presence. It was such a high level of peace and contentment. Even just to observe the sun shining through those stained windows, gave a real radiance of God's glory! This very act of worship is what prepared me for the upcoming assignments God had designed for me at that time.

In our same community, there was an elderly man that had been injured by a gunshot and he was very ill. Several times a week, I would stop by their home and pray for him in his bedroom. He wasn't bothered by the stuttering and no one would laugh. I was received with warm hearts and those prayers, I believe, were well received. As a young lad, in my own way, I felt blessed to be able to minister to him.

A couple of years later, my pastor wanted me to assist him and the deacons in serving communion to the members who were sick and shut-in. When some of the older mothers would see me coming, they would normally say, "Now here come my little preacher". Whether or not it was known to them, they were speaking faith into my life and made me aware that regardless of my imperfections, I still have hope.

It was then I realized that every moment of my life was a teachable moment that could impact me forever. Therefore, it is imperative that we never overlook anything that our God leads us into. God will use these situations to build us and make us stronger until we ultimately reach our greatest potential. But we have to recognize these moments and be willing to act on them.

The foundation of prayer and the support of my family were the fundamentals that were essential in my journey to restoration. These were the key components that empowered me to push through my difficulties. Knowing that God was always with me, even in my mistakes, was very encouraging. The more I felt God's presence and the love from my family, the more confident I became. I learned that I could pray to God and He wouldn't mind that I didn't have elegance of speech. However, He did need to know that my heart was connected to His.

Zechariah 4:10a, (MSG) Does anyone dare despise this day of small beginnings?

Chapter 3

Deliver the enemy from within

And when He had come out of the boat, immediately there met Him out of the tombs a man with an unclean spirit, who had his dwelling among the tombs; and no one could bind him, not even with chains,

Because he had often been bound with shackles and chains and the chains had been pulled apart by him, and the shackles broken in pieces; neither could anyone tame him.

And always, night and day, he was in the mountains and in the tombs, crying out and cutting himself with stones.

When he saw Jesus from afar, he ran and worshiped Him. And he cried out with a loud voice and said, "What have I to do with You, Jesus, Son of the Most High God? I implore You by God that You do not torment me."(NKJV) Mark 5:2-7

In the text, there are three different forces at work: Satan, Society, and our Savior. All three are extremely influential and can have the power tremendously impact your life negatively or positively if you allow them. It depends on which force you permit to be in the driver's seat. These same three forces are still at work in our world today, trying to control the lives of people. First, let us examine what **Satan** can do to people. He is a thief whose ultimate purpose is to destroy mankind.

"The thief cometh not, but for to steal, and to kill, and to destroy: I am come that they might have life, and that they might have it more abundantly". John 10:10

Demons are "unclean spirits" and can easily get a foothold in the lives of people who cultivate sinful practices. We are not told how or when the demons entered this man but they did and they took full control. Because he obviously yielded to Satan at some point, the thief has caused this man to lose everything! He lost his home as well as the fellowship with his family and friends. He also lost his dignity as he ran around in the tombs naked. He lost his self-control and lived like a wild animal; screaming, cutting himself, and frightening those that saw him. Additionally, he lost his peace and purpose for living, and he would have remained in that plight had Jesus not come through that storm to rescue him.

Jesus came through that storm for a man without a name or an e-mail address. His street address could have been a wild man in a dead man's location, a cemetery. So it is with many of us today. Many times we feel like a "nobody" and unimportant. Sometimes we are even bound and emotionally separated from the people around us. We even get weighted down by carrying dead things, emotions or relationships that are killing us inside. All alone and lost, we feel as though we just don't matter but this is truly a deception from the enemy. God knows how to find us just where we are because we matter to Him!

Do you not know there is no one or anything that can hold back the presence of our God from showing up on our behalf! Just when we need Him the most, He will always be there and never fail. Our God loves us so much that He does not want any of us wandering around in a cemetery or having dead things in our lives. While Satan, on the other hand, desires to always see us bound, in chains and in bondage.

Society will then add to our difficulties. There are people that have seen us in our graveyard condition, in chains, bound, and harming ourselves; yet they do nothing. They witness us in a critical condition and still make the conscious decision not to come to our aid. Often society will be like that priest in Luke 10; who saw the wounded man but passed by on the other side of the road. How about the Levite that came by after the priest, took the opportunity to look at him, but also passed by on the other side of the road? But thanks be to our God for that Good Samaritan, the one least expected to stop by, he gave him assistance and offered to pay the bill.

Our cemetery experience is just like that Jericho road experience. The obstacle is that society has the tendency to occasionally view it as the norm the more they witness us in our graveyard condition. Society will come to a place of complacency and we just become that condition in their eyes. Some determine that this is none of their business and then just disregard the entire event.

The chains could not hold this particular man because of the mental and demonic control on his life. It caused his strength to supersede the strength of the chains. Throughout the span of our lives, we have all had the opportunity to be around an individual that has had mental incapacities. On a rare occasion, I have personally observed that they can develop and utilize a powerful strength that even they were not aware they possessed. This type of bondage keeps a person from being in control of their mind and ultimately their destiny. Society has become desensitized to people experiencing a low place in their lives and will do very little to help them move from that place.

Occasionally society is content in knowing that we remain in that graveyard, in chains and naked. They find pleasure and satisfaction in knowing that we are broken! There are some people that don't want to see you healed, delivered and set free. Surprisingly, some of these people can be your closest friends or even your family. There is a spirit of jealousy suggesting that no one wants to see you doing well and if they had their way, the enemy would remain in control of our lives. Society will often aid in our bondage, unless God sends a Good Samaritan to you. I want to challenge you to become that Good Samaritan for someone else that may be in that same condition today.

What is your graveyard situation? What is keeping you surrounded by dead things that aren't producing positive outcomes in your life? What is holding you in that bound place that society comes to see as normal? What conditions in your life have you in bondage? What are you dealing with that causes others to pass by on the other side only to avoid getting involved in your situation?

I want you to know that God is taking you out of that graveyard condition right now! I decree and declare that those chains are falling off of you right now! Praise God in advance for being released from that state! After Satan gets through terrorizing, tormenting, laughing and scandalizing us; society will assist where the enemy leaves off. But I have news for you; we have a Savior that has come to give us life, an abundant life.

The **Savior** made a difference in his life! Jesus said unto him, "Come out of the man, thou unclean spirit". Then He asked him, "What is thy name?" and he answered saying, "My name is Legion; for we are many ". But the increase in number still was no match for our Lord. When Jesus speaks, everything must obey. The man was delivered and released from the unclean spirit, thus initiating his complete restoration.

What Jesus did for the unnamed man in that cemetery, he will do for each one of us as well. He will rescue us from our sinful state. Otherwise, the enemy that we allow to control us will continually cause us to lose even our hope and trust in God. I guess that's why I love that hymn that says; "I was sinking deep in sin far from the peaceful shore, very deeply stained within sinking to rise no more, but the Master of the sea heard my despairing cry, from the waters lifted me, now safe am I".

It was God's love that lifted me when nothing else would help. It was God's love that lifted all of us! God's love is an infinite fatherly warmth and affection towards sinners; it is immeasurable compassion. God's love is unutterably full, perfect, and blissful. Thank God for His amazing love.

One of our older church mothers once told me "Love is not real love until you give it away" God illustrated a perfect example of His love when He gave His Son Jesus to die on that cross for all of our sins.

Our Savior has made a difference, regardless of how Satan or Society has negatively impacted our lives. When the Lord shows up, something will have to happen. That unnamed man was completely restored. Earlier when people saw him, they were afraid and didn't offer any assistance. Perhaps they were afraid of how he looked; but Jesus looked beyond his appearance and his faults, then saw there was a need. After seeing the enemy within, He commanded that unclean spirit to come out of him. Jesus restored him and he looked brand new.

I am pronouncing unto you that those who are experiencing the enemy within you today; the enemy is coming out of you right now and you will become a new creature in Christ Jesus. First you must identify what your enemy is, be willing to leave that graveyard situation, and watch God work on your behalf. Jesus is the answer and only He will make the difference. My enemy was fear, uncertainty and a lack of confidence but I am so grateful for full restoration.

Therefore, if any man be in Christ, he is a new creature: old things are passed away; behold all things are become new. 2 Corinthians 5:17

Chapter 4

Laughing to Scorn

But thou, O LORD, shalt laugh at them; thou shalt have all the heathen in derision. Psalms 59:8 (KJV)

Having gone through what I've gone through, I absolutely understand what it is like to be laughed at and not necessarily laughed with. There is a difference you know? When considering the understanding of bullying today, I can relate to being mocked, joked, laughed at, or made fun of, which are all strong forms of bullying. Even though years ago, those things were never thought of in the same manner as bullying, it most definitely is. To some, certain individuals who had issues were never treated fairly their whole lives.

Since my childhood days, I have always been the one that would be drawn to the less fortunate, rather than one who would make fun of others. I never knew why people would be so cruel. Maybe it was because of their clothing, mental inabilities or physical handicaps. Nevertheless, they are like everyone else and they have feelings also. To laugh at people that have issues or misfortunes is wrong on every level. Can you begin to imagine that a group of bystanders even laughed at Jesus, the Christ? St. Mark recorded this incident of people laughing at Jesus out of their unbelief.

There are a few individuals that I have known since the first grade, who are alive today and are still in that unfortunate condition. The things that they encountered then and even now, I know they did not ask for it nor did they do anything to deserve it. I am where I am today because of the grace of God and we always need to know what the apostles, James and Peter, recorded in the word of God:

But he giveth more grace. Wherefore he saith, God resists the proud, but giveth grace unto the humble James 4:6 (KJV)

As every man hath received the gift, even so minister the same one to another, as good stewards of the manifold grace of God. 1Peter 4:10 (KJV)

Can you imagine anybody laughing at Jesus? What in the world were they thinking? Let us observe how John described who Jesus is:

In the beginning was the Word, and the Word was with God, and the Word was God. The same was in the beginning with God. All things were made by him; and without him was not anything made that was made. In him was life; and the life was the light of men. John 1:1-4 (KJV)

Let's look further at why they laughed at our Lord. Mark 5:40 states that they "laughed him to scorn". In the previous chapter, Jesus had already told them, let us pass over to the other side.

Well after that when the storm arose; He merely spoke three words, "Peace Be Still ", and there was peace. Perhaps He knew that on the other side, there was a woman that had an issue of blood, a problem she had for twelve years of her life that needed to be restored. On the other hand, there was a little girl that had only lived for twelve years and according to the scripture she had died, but had a father with so much faith that he believed God could bring her back to life.

*While he yet spake, there came from the ruler of the
synagogue's house certain which said, Thy daughter is
dead: why troublest thou the Master any further? 36 As
soon as Jesus heard the word that was spoken, he saith
unto the ruler of the synagogue, Be not afraid, only
believe. 37 And he suffered no man to follow him, save
Peter, and James, and John the brother of James. 38 And
he cometh to the house of the ruler of the synagogue, and
seeth the tumult, and them that wept and wailed greatly.
39 And when he was come in, he saith unto them, why
make ye this ado, and weep? the damsel is not dead,
but sleepeth. 40 And they laughed him to scorn. But
when he had put them all out, he taketh the father and
the mother of the damsel, and them that were with him,
and entereth in where the damsel was lying. 41 And he
took the damsel by the hand, and said unto her, Talitha
cumi; which is, being interpreted, Damsel, I say unto
thee, arise. 42 And straightway the damsel arose, and*

walked; for she was of the age of twelve years. And they were astonished with a great astonishment. 43 And he charged them straitly that no man should know it; and commanded that something should be given her to eat. Mark 5:35-43 (KJV)

"They laughed him to scorn"! First Jesus put them all out. Then he took the father and the mother of the damsel, and them that were with him, and entered in where the damsel was lying. He took control of the environment and made sure that it was right. In order for God to work efficiently in our lives, there are times that the Lord will encourage us to allow some folks who are experiencing doubt to leave, just so that God can do His work in our lives.

There will come a time in your life that you will have to put your doubters out from your home or possibly even your life. For somebody, you are at the very edge of your miracle; but just before that transpires, let's be sure that the atmosphere is conducive for that miracle to happen. It is imperative that you encircle your life with faith believing individuals! Your miracle depends on it.

Amongst all of the amazing facts about Jesus, I have found that He always kept His inner circle those who were closest to him, composed of individuals who were like-minded with himself. Normally when we read scripture; when a healing was being performed, souls were being delivered from demonic issues or a mountain top experience was to take place, especially experiences which were noteworthy and recorded from the inspired writers of scripture, three individuals were constantly mentioned. They were Peter, James and John. Jesus could depend on their faithfulness and consistence of heart. They always had a like disposition or purpose with Jesus.

Are there doubters and faith wavering individuals in your circle of friends? Do you have the correct team of believers in place in your life? Does your inner circle contain friends that impress and encourage you but at the same time can be honest and truthful with you? God is ready to work in your life. You and those that are in your circle must be willing to move beyond those that are only in your life to giggle gossip and gaze. What is their motive? Why are they with you? What do they really want from you? These are difficult questions that must be answered.

There are times that God will allow certain people to be in our lives, some just for a season and others to be that Judas. Encourage them to do what they do quickly because ultimately they are there to cause us to grow and complete our kingdom assignment. We know that nothing ever just happens by chance but everything in our lives happens for a reason.

My grandmother once asked me to borrow a particular item from a neighbor. This particular neighbor was someone that we would seldom borrow things from. I went inside of their home and stuttered so badly, that

I hardly got the words out. Once again, my mouth was open, but nothing but air came out. I finally managed to ask the request of my grandmother, however, they didn't have what my grandmother needed. I turned to leave and before I could close the door and leave the porch area, an enormous outburst of laughter which lasted for several minutes, came from the inside of that home. Several people were there at the time. I lowered my head and in disgust I walked back home. Until this day, I never told my family what had happened.

Regardless of how I had been treated, scorned or misunderstood; I never held that against them nor brought it up before them. I just loved and within my heart, forgave each of them. I have been laughed at, Jesus was laughed at to scorn, but there are two other types of laughter that I will present through Abraham and Sarah, who are classic examples to glean from.

Laughter of doubt

Now Abraham and Sarah were old and well stricken in age; and it ceased to be with Sarah after the manner of women, therefore Sarah laughed within herself, saying, after I am waxed old shall I have pleasure, my lord being old also? And the LORD said unto Abraham, wherefore did Sarah laugh, saying, Shall I of a surety bear a child, which am old?

Is anything too hard for the LORD? At the time appointed I will return unto thee, according to the time of life, and Sarah shall have a son. Genesis 18:11-14 (KJV)

As believers, we must be vigilant in what we say and do. For if we are not careful, we can laugh ourselves out of a miracle. God made a promise; nothing was going to deter the plans that God has for us. Never be skeptical of what the Lord can do for you. It is never too late to trust Him. Never doubt, for He will surely bring you out of any circumstance.

Laughter of Joy

Then Abraham fell upon his face, and laughed, and said in his heart, Shall a child be born unto him that is a hundred years old? And shall Sarah, that is ninety years old, bear? Genesis 17:17 (KJV)

Some people read this scripture and immediately assume that Abraham was doubtful and wavering in his faith. Let's consider the scripture in Romans 4:19-21:

And being not weak in faith, he considered not his own body now dead, when he was about an hundred years old, neither yet the deadness of Sara's womb: He staggered not at the promise of God through unbelief; but was strong in faith, giving glory to God; and being fully persuaded that, what he had promised, he was able also to perform.

Because of how the scripture speaks of Abraham's faith, it is highly unfeasible to believe that he laughed out of doubt. He laughed out of Joy, excited that God was getting ready to bless them with a son. Afterwards, God assured him that it was not Ishmael but his name would be Isaac. I believe that this is the kind of laughter, God is looking for and expecting from believers. He is not looking for one that scorns, jests, or doubts, but the kind of laughter that is joyous because of the assurance in knowing that the manifestation of an answered prayer and the fulfillment of the God's promises have come to fruition.

Chapter 5

Discovering the Treasure Inside

But we have this treasure in earthen vessels that the Excellency of the power may be of God, and not of us. We are troubled on every side, yet not distressed; we are perplexed, but not in despair; Persecuted, but not forsaken; cast down, but not destroyed, Always bearing about in the body the dying of the Lord Jesus, that the life also of Jesus might be made manifest in our body. 2 Corinthians 4:7-10 (KJV)

It does not matter what our lives have been like in the past. Regardless of whatever we've been through, nothing compares to what God has placed on the inside of us and it's all for our good! Jesus didn't come to put value in us, but He came so that we can recognize the value that is already inside of us. There is a treasure inside of you.

What others say about us should not be the compass for determining our ultimate value. When the word of God has been planted in us by someone sowing a seed of faith, then God will always have another individual add water to that seed; but at the end of the day, it is only God that can add the increase. Afterwards, He gets the Glory! Oh what a treasure that is on the inside of us right now!

How can I discover the treasure that is in me? I am so glad that you have asked that question. First of all, what is that treasure that the Apostle Paul asked about? The amplified bible describes it as "The divine light of the glorious gospel". According to Albert Barns NT commentary, the word "treasure" is applied to those truths on account of their inestimable worth. Paul, in the previous verses, had spoken of the gospel or the knowledge of Jesus Christ, as full of glory and infinitely precious.

That glorious gospel is inside of us as a treasure, but the only way to discover it is when our earthen vessel goes through the kiln or that fiery furnace of life. There is no other way for us to know the power of God, unless we experience that potter's touch while we are in the furnace.

I can now understand why the word of God says in 2 Corinthians 4:8, after it speaks about the treasure we have in earthen vessels, *"We are troubled on every side, yet not distressed; we are perplexed, but not in despair*". Why is this scripture of value to me? Perhaps because I have the power of God inside of me; but it's not about me, it is about God's word inside of me!

I believe that there are treasures inside of us but for the most part, we don't realize what our treasures really are. During my time of study, I have come to realize that sometimes God will allow our vessels to be jarred. Just know that when the Apostle Paul discussed vessels and treasures; of course our vessels are a demonstration of our bodies, while the treasure is in reality the word of God or the glorious gospel of Jesus Christ.

When our vessels get jarred, it has a propensity to get shaken up. Therefore, that treasure which is in us can spill over onto others. It just may spill over on your friend that hangs with you and perhaps they are the very one that needs it the most! This is one reason why God may allow this to happen in our life. It's not to harm us but to make us stronger and to be a benefit to those around us.

Recently I was led to deliver a message from a certain pericope. During the ending of the message, I had a water bottle in my hand to use as a visual demonstration of the vessel and the treasure. The water bottle was a representation of our vessels and the water inside was a representation of our treasure, or God's word. As I continued preaching, the bottle began to shake in my hand causing the water to spew over the brim. This signified the jarring and yes, when our vessels are jarred for some reason or another, the treasure could spill over on those next to you and be a tremendous blessing in their life. Unexpectedly, during the closing of the message, God's anointing was on me and I was led to use the water inside the water bottle to sprinkle on the believers. God used this illustration in a powerful way and the congregation was ultimately blessed!

Our treasure is also a result of what God has spoken into existence:

This treasure that is in us derived from our heavenly father, therefore from the beginning of time God has always been able to recognize and pull valuable treasures out of us.

What about Adam:

And the LORD God caused a deep sleep to fall on Adam, and he slept; and He took one of his ribs, and closed up the flesh in its place.

Then the rib which the LORD God had taken from man He made into a woman, and He brought her to the man.

And Adam said: "This is now bone of my bones and flesh of my flesh; she shall be called Woman, because she was taken out of Man." Genesis 2:21-23 (KJV)

Adam did not have any idea that he had such a treasure on the inside of him. Not only was Adam given supernatural ability to name all of the animals and to even have dominion over all of God's creations, but God pulled the woman out of him.

My first name is Theadore, but when the people spoke of me in a descriptive fashion, they would say: "you know, the boy that stutters and stammers". That is how people would refer to me, but at the end of the day, I know that the meaning of my name is “a gift of God”! This is how I chose to identify myself and I love that! So even though I stuttered and stammered; now knowing that my true identity was “a gift of God”, this was amazing to me! From that, I have come to realize that it is what God calls you that really matters.

What about Jacob? Jacob had to realize that there was something special on the inside of him. He had to live with the names that everyone had given him; a trickster, a heel holder, and a supplanter. Regardless of the many names that we may have been called, or are called today, it only makes a difference what God calls us.

During that era of time, an individual’s name reflected the type of person they were. This was true for Jacob because as you know; while he wrestled with the Angel Jehovah at Peniel, Jacob declared to him, “I won’t let you go until you bless me” When the wrestling match was completed, Jacob left with a limp, but the good news is that his name was changed from Jacob to Israel! Now his name is found in the Old and New Testament, illustrating the sovereignty of God and the power of faith. Isn’t it good to know that even though your given name meant one thing, after God’s intervention, you become one that prevails with God!

Before I end this section of discovering the treasure inside of you, I absolutely must suggest one of the most powerful women ever that transported a treasure. That woman would be Mary, the mother of Jesus. Do you recall how the angel of the Lord appeared unto Mary, a virgin, and told her that she would give birth to a son and his name shall be called Jesus? Can you imagine a conversation like that?

For with God nothing shall be impossible.

And Mary said, Behold the handmaid of the Lord; be it unto me according to thy word. And the angel departed from her.

And Mary arose in those days, and went into the hill country with haste, into a city of Juda; and entered into the house of Zacharias, and saluted Elizabeth.

And it came to pass, that, when Elizabeth heard the salutation of Mary, the babe leaped in her womb; and Elizabeth was filled with the Holy Ghost. Luke 1:37-41 (KJV)

This awesome treasure that was on the inside of the mother of Jesus has now impacted her cousin Elizabeth. The evidence of the greatness of that treasure is that it will also cause our treasure to leap. What a great connection we have today because of the presence and word of our God! For nine months, Mary carried that awesome gem inside of her, which was presented to her through the Holy Ghost.

And the angel answered and said unto her, the Holy Ghost shall come upon thee, and the power of the

Highest shall overshadow thee: therefore, also that holy thing which shall be born of thee shall be called the Son of God. Luke 1:35 (KJV)

But we have this treasure; the treasure of the gospel, which is the rich and invaluable truths in which the Apostles preached to others. The word "treasure" is applied to those truths. On account of their inestimable worth, our vessels are exalted by the treasure it contains. Paul compares the gospel he preached to a treasure. We contain this wealth and it is for the enriching and edifying of the church. The gospel is a treasure; for its worth and dignity, for its abundance and variety, and for its closeness and secrecy.

Inside of you rest a huge bundle of Joy. Just to think of it makes my treasure leap!

Chapter 6

Confidence

Confidence is self-assurance or the belief in your ability to succeed. It is also defined as the belief or trusts in somebody or something; or in the ability of that somebody or something to act in a proper, trustworthy, or reliable manner according to the Encarta Dictionary. All of these descriptions of confidence are what I knew I needed from God before the healing could take place in my life.

James 1:17 states that every good gift and every perfect gift is from above, and cometh down from the Father of lights with whom is no variableness, neither shadow of turning. I knew that whatever I needed in life, God has already provided it for me. Yet, somehow my level of confidence was still not very strong, perhaps the catalyst for this was my lack of acceptable speech. There was always a sense of inadequateness, so I tried to make it up by increasing my walk with God.

Christianity is not a mere religion that we practice but it is a confident way of living based on what God has done through Christ. I had to discover that my relationship with God had to be a way of life; therefore, as I continued to read God's word, this scripture began to resonate within me. The powerful phrase, "The just shall live by faith", is indicated four different times in four different books of God's word. I have come to realize that when God says something repeatedly in His word, that it must be very important to Him and that we should take heed. So that expression became the theme for my life.

Behold, his soul which is lifted up is not upright in him: but the just shall live by his faith. Habakkuk 2:4 (KJV)

For therein is the righteousness of God revealed from faith to faith: as it is written, the just shall live by faith. Romans 1:17(KJV)

But that no man is justified by the law in the sight of God, it is evident: for, the just shall live by faith. Galatians 3:11 (KJV)

Now the just shall live by faith: but if any man drawback, my soul shall have no pleasure in him. Hebrews 10:38 (KJV)

The more I read these scriptures, they became very important to me and I was beginning to believe that my faith, aligned with confidence, would be the key factor to my victory. Traveling for me was normally very limited; therefore, it basically consisted of church, school and work. At this point in my life, I had just graduated high school, was working at a great job and was beginning to feel comfortable within myself for who I was. Then months later, I was drafted into the military.

This began a period of many firsts in my life. It was my first time away from home, my first airplane ride, my first army base, and most definitely the first time that someone would look me in the face and tell me that they were going to be my momma, my daddy and my God. Having someone stand in front of me yelling and screaming was not normal life as I knew it. This atmosphere was not the same Christian home atmosphere that I grew up in and was accustomed to. So for those two years in the military, I stayed clear of trouble.

My first night in the barracks, while things were quiet, I could hear sniffing and crying from those grown young men. Little did I know that being drafted into the military would be so significant in our lives. As for my life, there was one question that surfaced to the forefront of my mind. Could this be the beginning of a breakthrough for me?

During the eight weeks of basic training, we were introduced to things that were designed to build confidence. We were trained on how to crawl under barbwire while tracer rounds of ammunition were being fired over us. We also mastered throwing hand grenades, climbing over walls, and climbing up ropes; all to give us confidence that we never thought we possessed. These were just a few of the things I accomplished that I had never experienced before.

After basic training was completed, promotions began to come. The basis for promotion was character, physical appearance, and your performance on a verbal and written test. While serving in the military, I was promoted from an E-1 to a Sergeant E-5 within eighteen months.

Upon the date of my departure from the military, I was promised that if I remained in the military, I would be guaranteed another promotion within months. I declined because I had a loving wife and a son to return to. It just wasn't the right move for me at that time but I do believe there was a divine purpose in my involvement in the military. Everything does happen for a reason.

For promotion cometh neither from the east, nor from the west, nor from the south, But God is the judge: he putted down one, and setteth up another. Psalms 75:6-7 (KJV)

I will always be grateful for my military experience, including the eleven months in Vietnam. One of the most important lessons this specific war has taught me is about God's omnipotence.

He is everywhere, all at the same time. Having that knowledge gave me a certain confidence that helped me to press forward through that period. I believe that confidence is a key factor for a turn-around in our lives and God used this military experience to grow my faith and confidence in Him. The more confident I felt, the less I stuttered and the more I knew God was with me in every situation, the more my life began to exude a solid foundation of faith.

Noticeably, the stuttering and stammering was beginning to cease. But when I returned home to my familiar surroundings, the stuttering returned and became heavier again. I have always heard this phrase: "Familiarity Breeds Contempt."

He came to His hometown and began teaching them in their synagogue, so that they were astonished, and said, "Where did this man get this wisdom and these miraculous powers? 55 "Is not this the carpenter's son? Is not His mother called Mary, and His brothers, James and Joseph and Simon and Judas? 56 "And His sisters, are they not all with us? Where then did this man get all these things?" 57 And they took offense at Him. But Jesus said to them, "A prophet is not without honor except in his hometown and in his own household." 58 And He did not do many miracles there because of their unbelief. Matthew 13:54-58 (KJV)

Jesus had difficulty when he was in His hometown, therefore, my life should not be any different. When attempting to do minor repairs to my vehicles, there was often a need to order parts. I recall making a call to the parts department and having a very difficult time saying anything. The salesman became agitated and passed the phone to someone else. I could hear him say, "Some guy on the line can't talk and I don't have time to wait, furthermore, I can't understand what he's saying". There were times when I just became exasperated with myself and wanted to give up on life.

On the weekends, we would go out to dinner as a family. Occasionally, we would go to a drive through and I would have to lean my body back so that my wife would place the order for us.

My wife would also have to complete sentences that I had started. Sometimes I managed to complete them myself, but only with the help of God! I often thought about Moses' condition and how he complained to God about his slow speech. God comforted him by letting him realize that Aaron was there as a backup plan. My wife was the backup plan for me until He healed me. Even then, God had me covered; therefore, my confidence always remained in Him. Our confidence in Christ does not make us negligent or careless, but on the contrary it awakens us, urges us on, and makes us active in living righteous lives and doing well.

Now this is the confidence that we have in Him, that if we ask any thing according to His will, he hears us: And if we know that He hears us, whatsoever we ask, we know that we have the petitions that we have asked of Him. 1 John 5:14-15 (NKJV)

This word of God lets me know that when our prayers are rendered, they are connected to our level of faith. With the level of difficulty my life was enduring, my mind was determined that my faith had to catch up to the desires of my heart.

Delight thyself also in the LORD; and he shall give thee the desires of your heart. Psalms 37:4(KJV)

When I read that scripture, I knew this was one of the most important desires of my life, at least at that time. I was tired and weary of the way my life was and had no idea that one part of my brokenness could hugely impact so much of my entire life. I knew how to pray and I thought I knew how to trust God, but I wasn't really serious about applying God's word to my life. It's called life application. When the text says "He will give us the desires of our heart", I had to know that the prayers we pray must be aligned with the will of God; without a doubt, without wavering, while fully trusting that He was hearing and answering my prayers. I knew the importance of having confidence, but I needed to know how to apply that which I have read into my life experiences.

It is better to trust in the LORD than to put confidence in man. Psalms 118:8 (KJV)

This was just the opposite for me. I was placing more confidence in people, trusting what they could and would do for me, rather than God. When we put our trust in man and it doesn't work out, it tends to make us mean, grouchy and irritable; but when we put our confidence in God,

He elevates us and produces a sacred quiet spirit and ultimately sanctifies the soul.

It is far better to trust in God, than man. Just look at *Ephesians 3:20* which Pronounce: *"Now unto Him that is able to do exceeding abundantly above all that we ask or think, according to the power that works in us"*. Our confidence in God makes us sure of ourselves. It makes us better, wiser, morally right, and blessed in every possible way of life.

Chapter 7

Divine Healing

The steps of a good man are ordered by the LORD: and He delights in his way. Psalms 37:23 (NKJV)

Our entire lives have been orchestrated from the first day of conception. Romans 8:28; naturally every born again believer already knows what this scripture implies, but how many of you really have lived this scripture? It says, *"And we know that all things work together for good to them that love God, to them who are the called according to his purpose*".

The things that I have gone through were not accidental, but they were intentional; and what I've been through was not intended to hurt or harm me, but to bless me. For years the church family would pray for me. My family would also be in prayer for me that the stammering and stuttering would stop, but seemingly all to no avail.

During the early days of my life while I was serving as a deacon, there were several individuals who mistakenly thought I was the pastor, can you believe that? During a revival service, an evangelist was praying for me and said "You are behind in accordance to where God intended for you to be, therefore it is time to accept the call that God has for you". I knew the statement was true, but at the moment I did not feel that it was my time. I did not know how God was going to fix me, but I knew in my heart that He would eventually do just that.

Old wives' tales are often passed on to others as solutions on how to fix things. One of them was a remedy to stop stuttering. The instructions were to place a dirty dishrag in your mouth and that was supposed to be the cure for it. My mother and grandmother did not believe that for one moment, so they just quietly believed God.

To some, stuttering was very comical. As a matter of fact, during that era of time, comedians were making a fortune imitating stuttering and being intoxicated.

I went to work as normal, fulfilling the assignment on my job, but little did I know that God was preparing the normal and the natural events of my life to make a change for my good.

One Wednesday night while I was working the second shift at E.I. DuPont as the relief operator, my assignment was to relieve three employees for their break and lunch periods. This was the last relief break for the night and the person I was relieving returned from his lunch. I attempted to explain the problem that I had with the machine while he was away.

He stood there and never chuckled or laughed at me, but just watched my opened mouth with nothing coming out but air. I knew he was friends with individuals that were considered popular and I felt like he was going to burst out into laughter at any moment.

My anxiety was building and my nervousness was increasing, but I finally got enough information out so he could understand what I was trying to say. I walked away and isolated myself in the men's restroom where I began praying to God. There was an hour left before going home for the night. In that moment, praying to God was the only thing on my mind. So every chance I had for the rest of the evening, I prayed.

Ask, and it will be given you; seek, and you will find; knock and it will be opened to you: For everyone who asks receives and he who seeks finds and to him who knocks it will be opened. Matthew 7:7-8 (NKJV)

My speech was flawed, but I knew enough scripture to begin believing what it meant to ask God in prayer, to seek Him, to knock and it would be opened. Always prepared to receive whatever God had to give, I was ready to inhale what God was ready to exhale into me. We should always be open, willing and available to God.

I am the LORD thy God, which brought thee out of the land of Egypt, open thy mouth wide and I will fill it. Psalms 81:10 (KJV)

God brought the Israelites out of bondage and He only required that they opened their mouths wide and He was ready to fill it! God, my mouth is open, and I need you to fill it with your glory and fill it with your healing touch. Pour into me Lord, for only what I receive from you will cause a change in my dismal situation.

My expectation of God was that He had to do something but questions still remained within me. Did I believe what I was reading? Would God actually heal me when I asked Him? My mouth was open wide to receive, I was seeking and knocking, but is God really going to respond to my needs?

At that moment, I was at the point of desperation. I couldn't wait to leave my job, get in my car and drive home! After leaving work and just before I arrived home, I stopped the car to earnestly seek the face of the Lord. This was a pivotal moment in my life. The intensity of my prayer indicated that I was finished with this traumatic speech issue and my conversation to God was that I refused to attempt to say another word to anybody until you healed me from this.

My wife had to go to work the next morning, so after I got home from work that night, I decided to just ease into bed without disturbing her. I didn't want to wake her up for fear of being asked a question, because I was now determined not to say a word to anyone until God heals me! The next morning, when my wife woke up to go to work, I was awake but did not want her to know it; so I laid there quietly with my head covered.

After my wife left for work, I got up and fell directly on my knees and began praying, still refusing to speak to anyone until I was healed. Enough was just enough. I had made up my mind that God would have to do something for me. I was at home alone and all day I prayed to God. I began to pray out loud and guess what? Remarkably by that evening, I did not stutter or stammer in my praying.

I went back to work, talked to guys on the job and didn't stutter. The next morning, I spoke to my wife and she noticed that the stuttering was gone. It was as if I had a new voice and speech. I was excited beyond measure. One of our neighbors noticed my speech and voiced with amazement, "You don't sound like yourself; the sound of your voice was as if you have lived in another city, what happened"?

I absolutely knew it was God and not man. God's healing power was imparted into my life and divine healing had taken place. Knowing that there was a call on my life, the enemy never wanted me to know what God had placed on the inside of me.

I was ready to put the past in the past and look forward to seeing what the future had in store for me. Looking back; even though I was able to serve as an ordained deacon, this assignment required minimal conversation. However, my speech difficulty had been holding back the ultimate destiny of my life, but this was not the case any longer. Not only did God heal me, but He was now beginning to put me in positions that required effective speech.

Destiny was being restored into my life. I can now order my own food at the drive through, or speak to anyone comfortably without the fear of stuttering or stammering. With all the thoughts that come to mind concerning my speech difficulty, one thing remains at the heart of the matter; and that is, from the moment that the stuttering ended, my life took a turn and my destiny began to unfold.

The job I held at DuPont at that time was an isolated position. It was an assignment that required me to work alone, but God was hiding me until the proper time. I will never forget this; one-night God gave me a dream and told me which job to apply for, the next day I followed His instructions.

A few years later after following the instructions from the Lord, I became a supervisor within that area, then a trainer for employees, including newly hired individuals. All of these positions were ones which required me to be able to speak clearly. Before I retired from DuPont, I was promoted to several positions which often required speaking with area managers, including our plant manager. My speech was no longer hindering my advancement and I was able to move forward.

Not only did God heal me for the purpose of improved job opportunities, but there was this call of God in my life. Years after God healed me, I was licensed as a minister and three years following that, I was ordained as an assistant pastor of our church. Then after pastoring for twenty-four years, I was consecrated as Bishop. None of this would have happened if God had not restored my brokenness!

Today I have been preaching the gospel for thirty-three years. There have been times the enemy tried to pull me back to those days of old, but God reminds me of whose I am and keeps me focused on what He has already done for me. Therefore, I know, "*I can do all things through Christ which strengthens me*".

Brethren, I count not myself to have apprehended; but one thing I do, forgetting those things which are behind and reaching forward to those things which are ahead. Philippians 3:13 (NKJV)

God is so good. He is our Jehovah Nissi, which means our banner or our God that goes before us. Whenever there is a battle that we are confronted with, He will move ahead of us and conquer those battles. He is Jehovah Rapha, which means the God who heals us! The angels of the Lord surround us and will inevitably look out for our good. Because God healed me from one thing, I believe He can heal me of other illnesses as well.

He heals the brokenhearted, and binds up their wounds Psalms 147:3 (NKJV)

The reason for our declaring his praise is due to the fact that the Lord is not only a builder and creator, but a healer. He restores broken hearts and anything that has been destroyed by the enemy! The Lord is constantly healing and binding, this is not new work for Him. He has done it repeatedly since the beginning of time. He is alpha and omega, the beginning and the end; and He is still healing and still binding today.

Casting all your care upon Him; for He cares for you 1 Peter 5:7(NKJV)

Thank God for that word because now we won't have to live an isolated life. All of us can come to Him with our brokenness; our broken hearts, broken dreams, broken marriages, or failed health. Today we can go to the great physician who never fails to heal. Allow Him to uncover your wounds, so He can then tenderly bind them up!

God's divine healing and restoration continues....

My faith was encouraged and the word hope came alive when I realized it was God that healed me from my stuttering tongue. The Greek word for healing is *iaomai* which means cured, or in other words, made whole. God doesn't just want to heal part of us, but it is His desire to make us whole. I am so grateful that God wasn't finished with me after he healed my speech because there were still other parts of me that were broken.

Approximately twenty years ago, I had severe pain in my left shoulder when attempting to elevate my arm. After making an appointment with my doctor, it was requested that I have X-Rays and MRI testing done. It was discovered that my vertebrae was causing a problem with my spinal cord. This was causing the weakness during walking and at that time explained the reason for the pain in my left shoulder.

I was told that I needed surgery immediately on my vertebrae and spinal cord. The doctors began to explain the procedure but I clearly heard the voice of God say, "NO"! The doctors continued discussing the necessity of having this surgery to make sure that I clearly understood the severity of the situation. I asked if I come back later in order to have a couple months to consider having this procedure done. They replied, "Within six months, you would not be able to walk at all"; therefore, I would have to agree to this surgery immediately. They informed me that it was either now or never, and later would be too late. I decided to listen to the voice of God and not have that surgery. As a result, twenty years later I am still walking two miles at a time. It's not too fast but I am continually walking steady; more importantly, walking by faith!

Several months ago, history repeated itself. Again I was informed that I needed surgery in that same area; and even worse, there was a possibility of cancer there also. Needless to say, adequate testing including X-Rays, MRI's and bone scans were performed. The results were conclusive, “NO CANCER”. Also, the doctor did not believe surgery was required at this time. Praise God!

God is still in the healing business. He is still restoring His children back to the place of victory, a place where we will have sight of our destiny. Because of our Lord and Savior, Jesus Christ, there is hope. All throughout time, God has healed many who had the faith to believe and He will do the same now that He has done in the past!

In conclusion

Thank you for reading this book. It was written from the table of my heart and the story is still unfolding. This book represents a major part of my life’s history. For me, it was my brokenness of speech that God mended. If you know anyone else that may have been experiencing the same or any difficulty and have yet to be restored, please share this book with them and my prayer is that they would be restored by the awesome hand of God!

Regardless of the difficulty or problems that life has handed many of us, God is able and willing to restore us to our intended place in life. If you think that God cannot heal you, just know that if He did it for me, I know that He can do it for you also. I have seen it happen.

www.ingramcontent.com/pod-product-compliance
Lightning Source LLC
Chambersburg PA
CBHW021345060726
47591CB00006B/2175

* 9 7 8 1 9 7 1 6 0 1 2 0 5 *